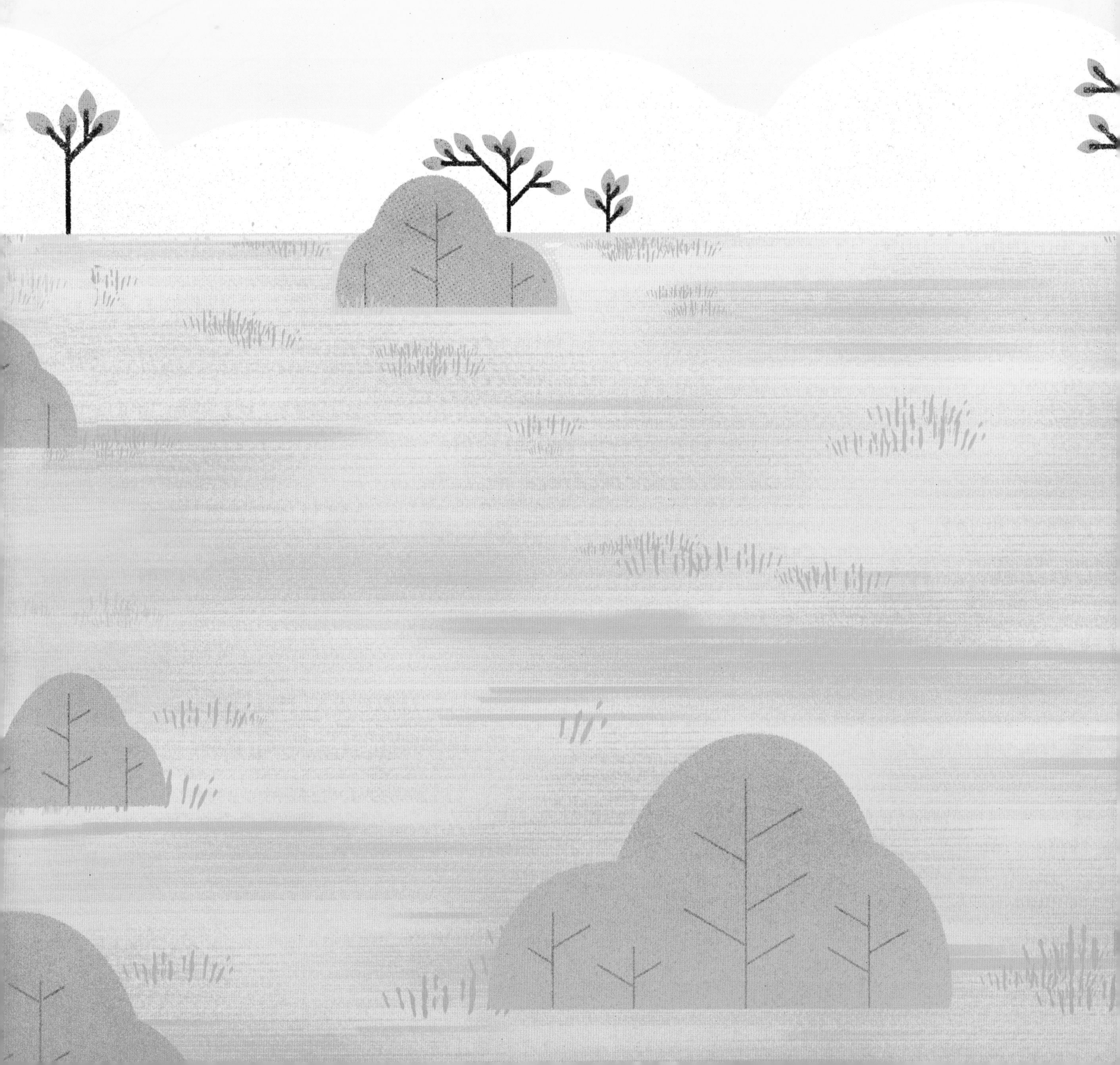

Customer Service: 1-877-277-9441 or customerservice@pikidsmedia.com

Published by Phoenix International Publications, Inc.

8501 West Higgins Road   59 Gloucester Place
Chicago, Illinois 60631   London W1U 8JJ

PI Kids and *we make books come alive* are trademarks of Phoenix International Publications, Inc., and are registered in the United States.

www.pikidsmedia.com

8 7 6 5 4 3 2 1

ISBN: 978-1-5037-5248-1

Wild Goose Chase

Funny Animal Phrases and the Meanings Behind Them

Written by Kathy Broderick
Illustrated by Dragan Kordić

we make books come alive®
Phoenix International Publications, Inc.
Chicago • London • New York • Hamburg • Mexico City • Sydney

wild goose chase

definition : a difficult and long search for something that is not important or that cannot be found

raining cats and dogs

definition : raining very hard

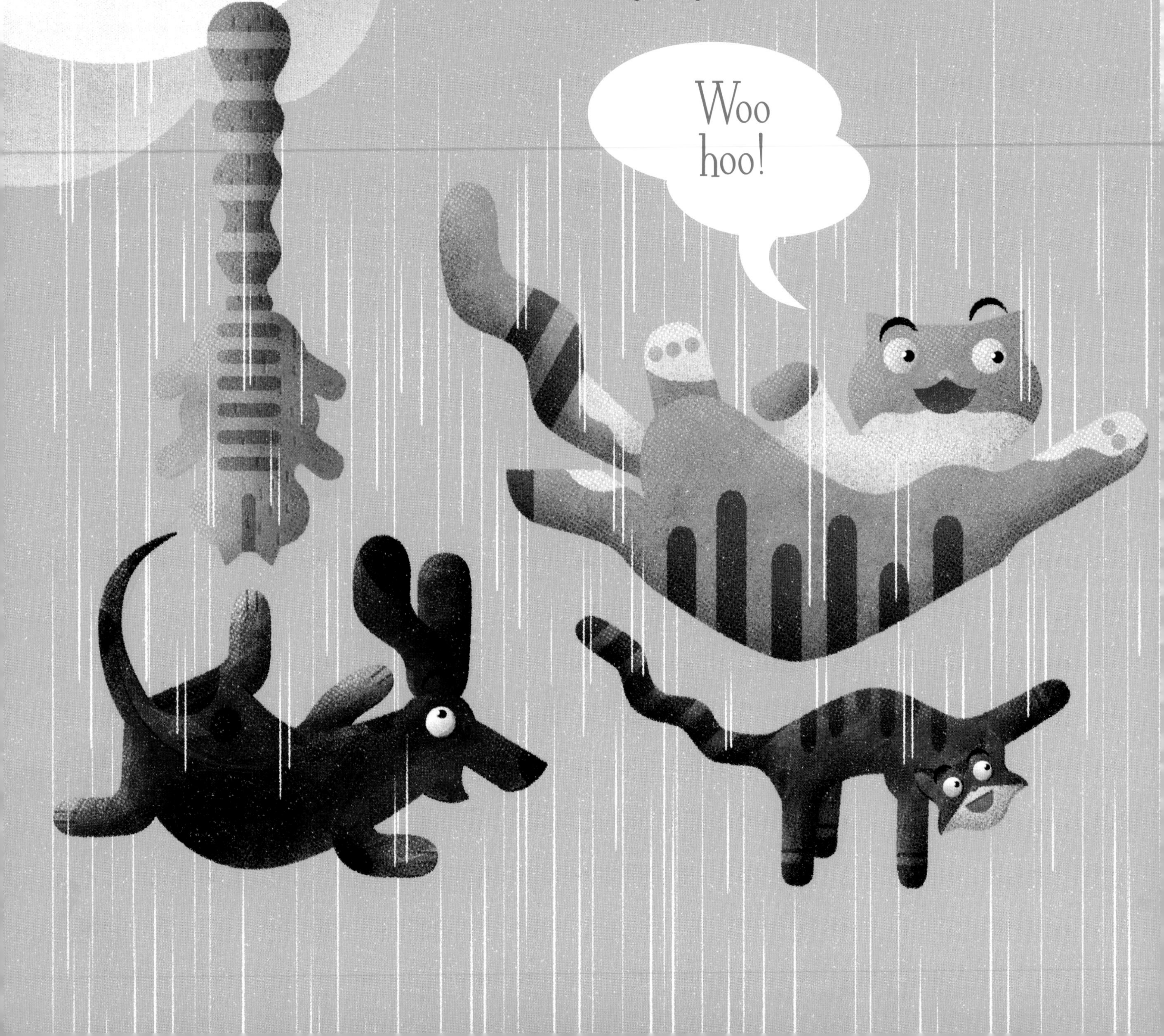

elephant in the room

definition : an obvious and important problem
or issue that people avoid mentioning

Oh, just pretend
I'm not here.

when pigs fly

definition : never—used when you
think something will never happen

Wheeee!

monkey around

definition : to do things that are not useful or serious; to waste time

fish out of water

definition : a person who is in a place or situation that seems unnatural or uncomfortable

snake in the grass

definition : a person who tells lies and betrays other people

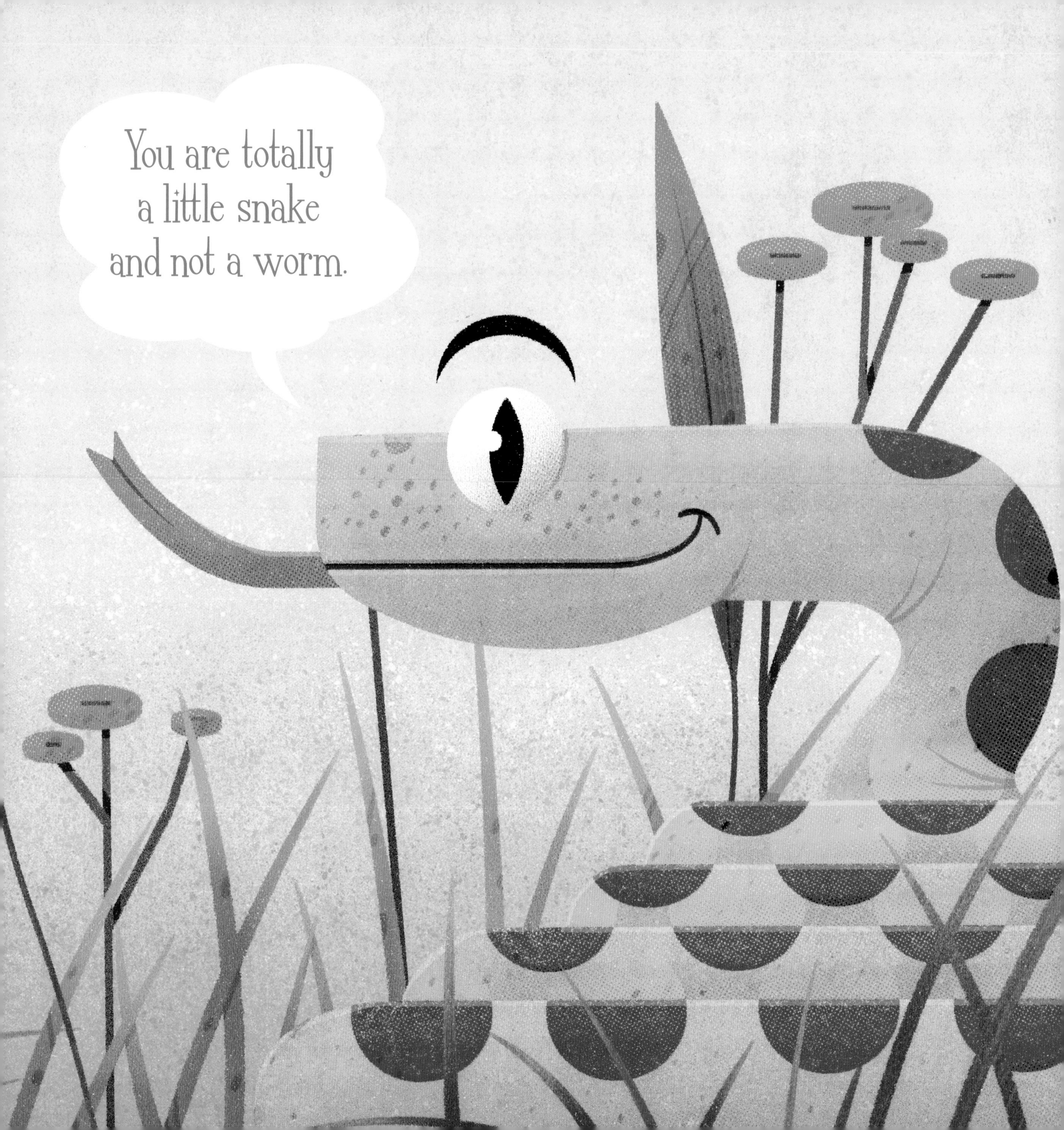
You are totally a little snake and not a worm.

ants in your pants

definition : a strong feeling of wanting to be active and not wait for something; a feeling of excitement and impatience

wolf in sheep's clothing

definition : a person who appears to be friendly or helpful but who really is dangerous or dishonest

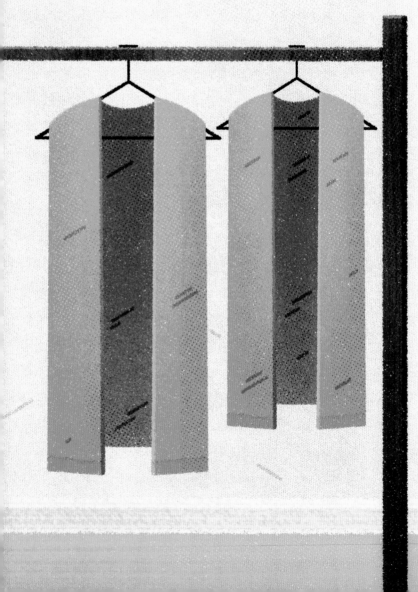

Is wool a good look for me?

crocodile tears

definition : a false expression of
sadness or regret about something

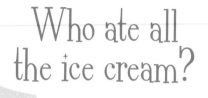

put the cart before the horse

definition : to do things in the wrong order; to do something first instead of waiting until something else has been done

fly in the ointment

definition : someone or something that causes problems

ruffle some feathers

definition : to upset or offend someone

can of worms

definition : a complicated situation in which doing something to correct a problem leads to many more problems

until the cows come home

definition : for a very long time

let the cat out of the bag
definition : to reveal a secret